Unofficial Math Adventures for
HARRY POTTER FANS
Addition & Subtraction
Grades 1-2

Sky Pony Press
New York

Sky Pony Press books may be purchased in bulk at special discounts for sales promotion, corporate gifts, fund-raising, or educational purposes. Special editions can also be created to specifications. For details, contact the Special Sales Department, Sky Pony Press, 307 West 36th Street, 11th Floor, New York, NY 10018 or info@skyhorsepublishing.com.

Sky Pony® is a registered trademark of Skyhorse Publishing, Inc.®,
a Delaware corporation.

Visit our website at www.skyhorsepublishing.com.

10 9 8 7 6 5 4 3 2 1

Cover design by Kai Texel
Cover art by Amanda Brack
Interior artwork by Shutterstock
Book design by Noora Cox

Print ISBN: 978-1-5107-6026-4

Printed in China

A NOTE TO PARENTS

When you want to reinforce classroom skills at home, it's crucial to have kid-friendly learning materials. This *Unofficial Math Adventures for Harry Potter Fans* workbook transforms math practice into a magical adventure complete with wizards, wands, and messenger owls. That means less arguing over homework and more fun overall.

Unofficial Math Adventures for Harry Potter Fans is also fully aligned with National Common Core Standards for 1st and 2nd grade math.

As the workbook progresses, the math problems become more advanced. Encourage your child to progress at his or her own pace. Learning is best when students are challenged, but not frustrated. What's most important is that your little wizard is engaged in his or her own learning.

Whether it's the joy of seeing their beloved book characters on every page or the thrill of solving challenging problems just like Harry and his friends, there is something in this workbook to entice even the most reluctant math student.

Happy adventuring!

ADDITION BY GROUPING

Circle groups of 10. Then count and write the numbers.

Example:

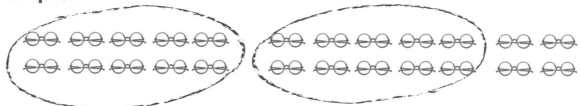

Answer: **24**

1.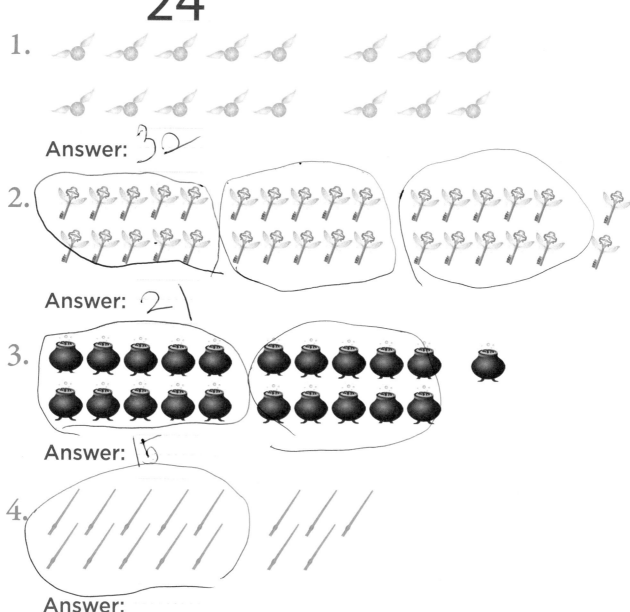

Answer: 30

2.

Answer: 21

3.

Answer: 15

4.

Answer:

MYSTERY MESSAGE

Add or subtract. Then use the letters to fill in the blanks below and reveal the answer to Hermione's joke.

4 + 8 = **12 D**   8 – 2 = **6 R**

6 – 3 = **3 O**   9 + 6 = **15 B**

3 + 8 = **11 O**   10 – 3 = **7 L**

7 – 5 = **2 C**   5 + 9 = **14 E**

8 + 5 = **13 U**   5 + 5 = **10 S**

Q: Why do Slytherins cross the road twice?

A: Because they are...

Copy the letters from the answers above to hear the punchline.

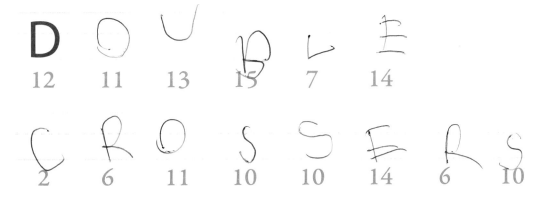

D   O   U   B   L   E
12   11   13   15   7   14

C   R   O   S   S   E   R   S
2   6   11   10   10   14   6   10

5

HARRY'S GUIDE TO PLACE VALUE

Use the number on each scarf to fill in the place value chart.

Example:

Tens	Ones
2	6

1.

Tens	Ones
4	2

2.

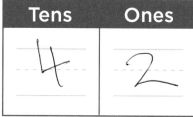

Tens	Ones
3	5

3.

Tens	Ones
3	7

4.

Tens	Ones
1	8

5.

Tens	Ones
4	4

6.

Tens	Ones
2	9

SKIP COUNT CHALLENGE

Count by 2s and fill in the empty spaces to reach the goblet of fire and compete in the wizard tournament.

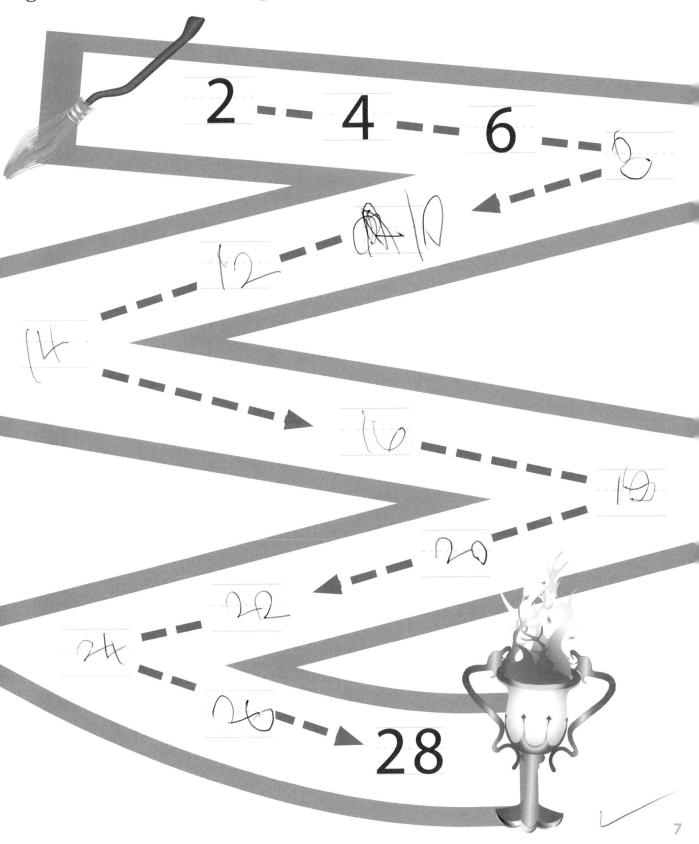

2 - 4 - 6 - 8 - 10 - 12 - 14 - 16 - 18 - 20 - 22 - 24 - 26 - 28

TELLING TIME

Weird clocks.

Look at the clocks below and write the time in the space provided:

Example:

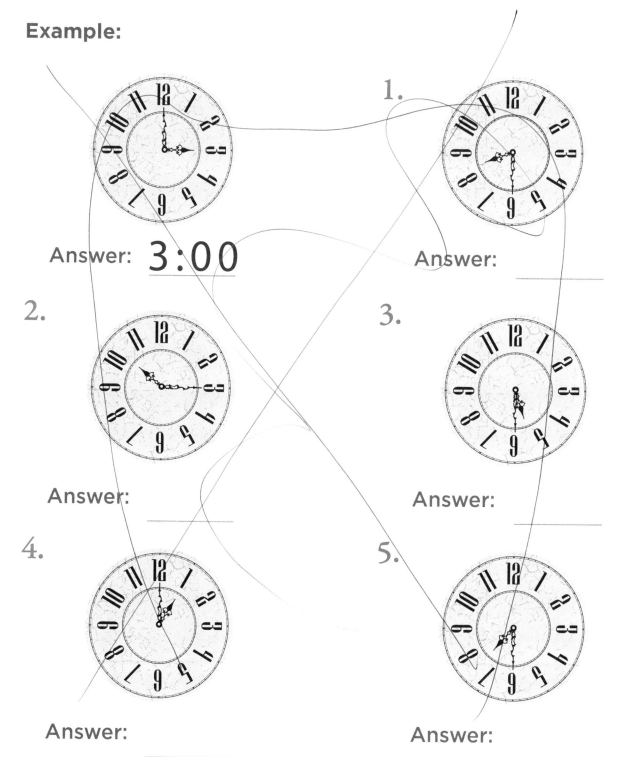

Answer: **3:00**

1.

Answer: _____

2.

Answer: _____

3.

Answer: _____

4.

Answer: _____

5.

Answer: _____

8

COUNTING MONEY

You're saving up for a brand new wand. Add your coins to see how much money you have.

25¢   10¢   5¢   1¢

Example: 25¢ + 20¢ + 10¢ + 5¢ = **60¢**

1. 10¢ + 5¢ + 1¢ + 1¢ + 1¢ =

2. 15¢ + 10¢ + 1¢ =

3. 25¢ + 45¢ + 5¢ + 5¢ =

4. 10¢ + 10¢ + 1¢ + 1¢ =

5. 25¢ + 5¢ + 5¢ =

6. 50¢ + 1¢ + 1¢ + 1¢ + 1¢ =

WIZARD CHALLENGE: *Try this advanced problem!*

It costs 45¢ for a bag of chocolate flavor beans. How many (5¢) nickels do you need to buy a bag?

Answer:

9

ADVENTURES IN GEOMETRY

Let's learn about fractions! Count the number of squares below.

Example:

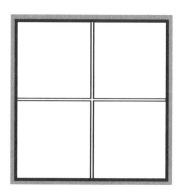 4

1. Color 1 of the 4 squares red.

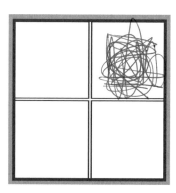

This is called one fourth, or ¼.

 $\frac{1}{4}$

2. This magic chest is divided into 2 equal parts. Color 1 of the 2 parts yellow.

This is called one half, or ½.

 $\frac{1}{2}$

3. Count the rectangles in the bar below.
   Write the number here: _9_

4. This bar is divided into 3 equal parts.
   Color 1 part green.

This is called one third, or ⅓.

5. This bar is divided into 3 equal parts.
   Color 2 parts green.

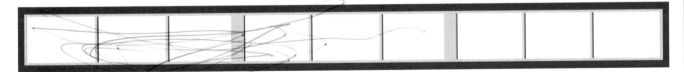

This is called two thirds, or ⅔.

WIZARD CHALLENGE: *Try this advanced problem!*

Color in 5 of the thunderbolts below.

Circle the fraction that describes how many are colored in:

A. ½   B. ¼   C. ⅓

WORD PROBLEMS

Read the problem carefully. Use the picture to help you solve the problem. Fill in your answer.

Example:

You've been riding the Hogwarts Express to school for 7 minutes. It takes 10 minutes to get to school. How many minutes of your ride are left?

$$XXXXXX\square\square\square$$

10 – 7 =   **3**   Answer: **3 minutes**

1. You need 6 friends to play quidditch. You get 2 friends to join you. How many more friends do you need?

Answer:

2. You dig up 10 potted mandrakes. Only 8 of them cry out. How many mandrakes are silent?

Answer:

3. You find 6 spell books at Hogwarts. You take 2 of them home with you over break. How many are left?

Answer:

4. Harry has 7 pairs of glasses. He finds 2 more under his bed. How many pairs of glasses does Harry have?

Answer:

5. You receive 4 letters by owl. You get 4 more. How many letters do you have?

Answer:

6. There are 8 dragons chasing you. You defeat 3 of them. How many dragons are still chasing you?

Answer:

7. Yesterday you found 3 magic cauldrons. Today you found 8. How many more cauldrons did you find today?

Answer:

WIZARD'S GUIDE TO PLACE VALUE

Read the number on each phoenix to fill in the place value chart. Then, write the number in tally marks.

Example:

Tens	Ones
2	4

1.

Tens	Ones

2.

Tens	Ones

3.

Tens	Ones

4.

Tens	Ones

5.

Tens	Ones

6.

Tens	Ones

SKIP COUNT CHALLENGE

Wizard school is starting soon. Count by 5s and fill in the spaces to find your way to platform 9 ¾.

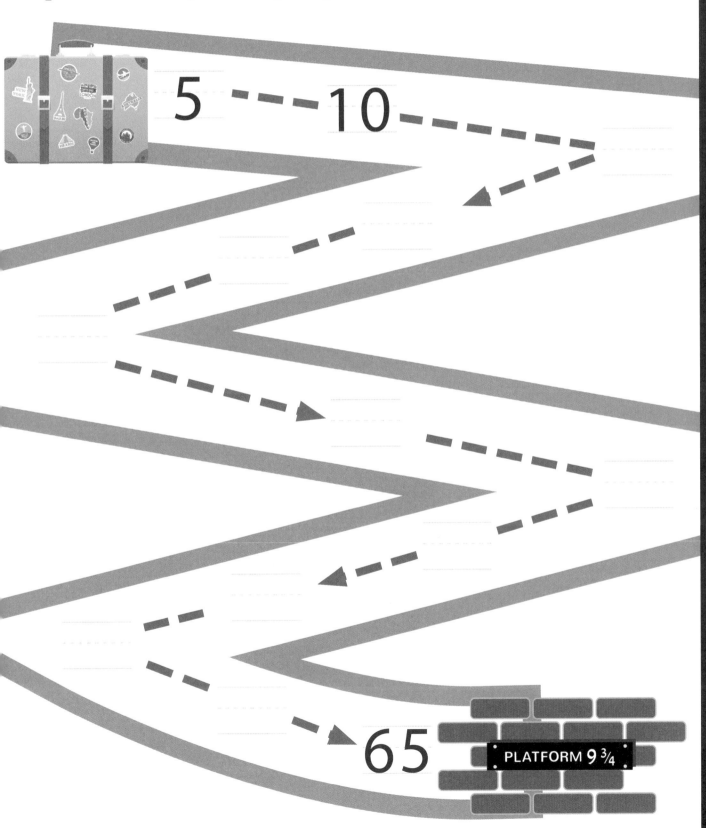

5 ---- 10

65

PLATFORM 9 ¾

TIME FOR MAGIC

A wizard's day is very busy! Match the time for each task on the left with a clock on the right.

Example:

6:00
Put on a tie.

 (A clock face)

A.

1.

7:30
Put on your cloak.

B.

2.

9:00
Brew a potion.

C.

3.

10:00
Play quidditch.

D.

4.

2:30
Fix your broomstick.

E.

5.

8:00
Escape Voldemort.

F.

6.

8:30
Enjoy some butterbeer.

G.

TELLING TIME

Draw a big hand and a little hand
on each clock to show the time.

Example:

3:00

1.

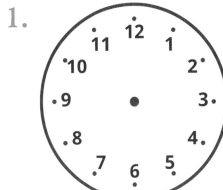

4:30

2.

2:00

3.

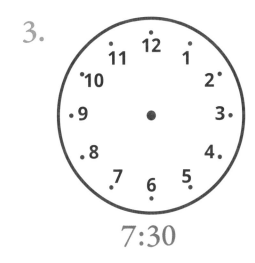

7:30

4.

10:15

5.

5:30

LEARNING ABOUT SHAPES

Draw along the dotted line to complete each shape. Connect the name of the shape to the correct drawing.

1. **Rectangle** A.

2. **Square** B.

3. **Trapezoid** C.

4. **Triangle** D.

FIND THE SHAPES

Look at the items below and and write the shape(s) you see in the picture. Use R for rectangle, C for circle, and T for triangle.

RECTANGLE	CIRCLE	TRIANGLE

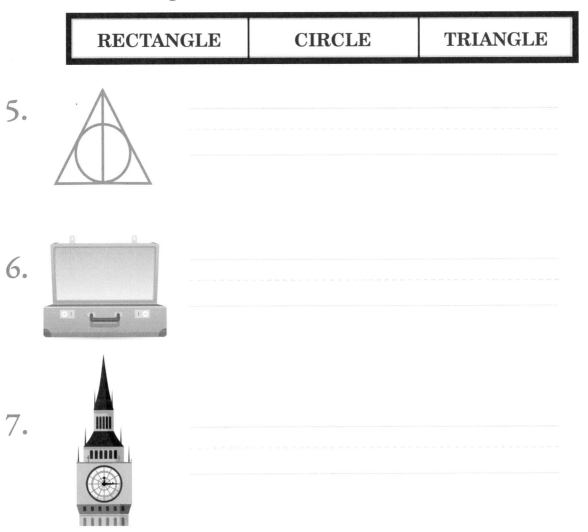

5.

6.

7.

WIZARD CHALLENGE: *Try this advanced problem!*

Draw your own ancient wizard symbol below. Include 3 shapes in your picture.

ADDITION BY GROUPING

Circle groups of 10 magical items. Then count and write the total number.

Example:

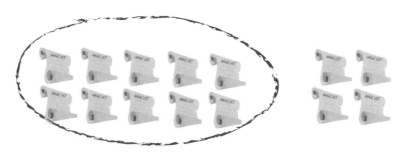

Answer: **14**

1.

Answer:

2.

Answer:

3.

Answer:

MYSTERY MESSAGE

Add or subtract. Then use the letters to fill in the blanks below and reveal the answer to Ron's joke.

12 + 8 = **20** H

16 + 3 = E

11 – 8 = A

19 – 5 = B

14 + 3 = Y

20 – 7= T

18 – 3 = D

13 – 2 = W

17 - 9 = O

15 - 8 = I

Q: Why didn't the wizard with the invisibility cloak go to the party?

Copy the letters from the answers above to find out.

H H   N
20   19   20   3   15   18   8

   14   8   15   17   13   8

G   H
16   8   11   7   13   20

THE TRIWIZARD CUP CHALLENGE

Match the goblet on the right with the description of the number.

Example:

Tens	Ones
2	4

A.
47

1.

Tens	Ones
4	3

B.
56

2.

Tens	Ones
5	6

C.
72

3.

Tens	Ones
4	7

D.
24

4.

Tens	Ones
7	2

E.
43

SKIP COUNT CHALLENGE

Count by 10s to help the unicorn get home to the Forbidden Forest.

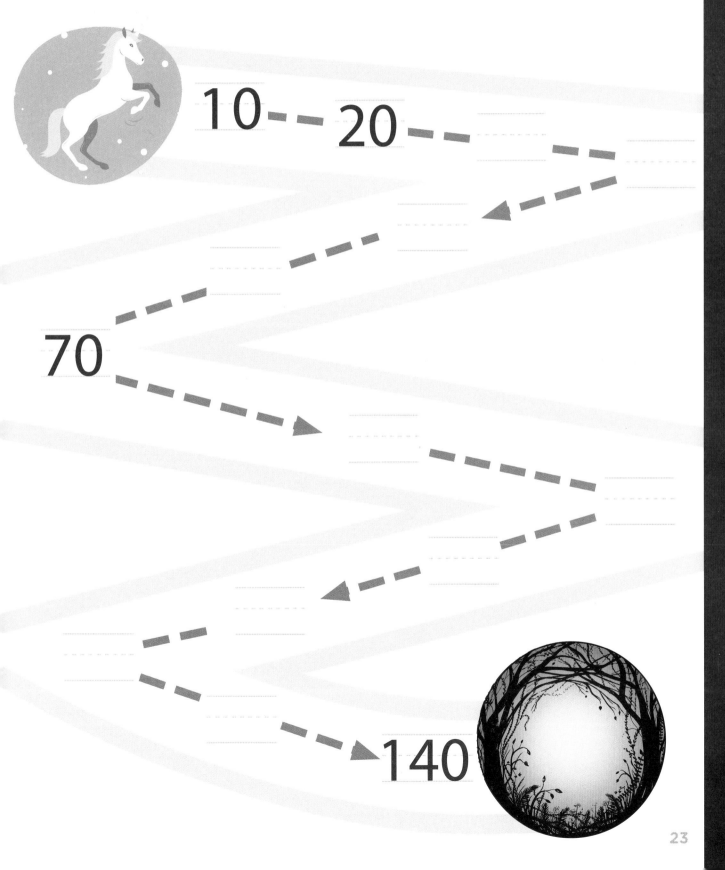

10 - - 20

70

140

MATH FACTS
FOR MUGGLES

Solve the math facts equations below.

PRACTICE YOUR ADDITION!

1. **5 + 5 =**

2. **5 + 2 =**

3. **3 + 5 =**

4. **6 + 2 =**

5. **8 + 2 =**

6. **4 + 5 =**

7. **3 + 7 =**

8. **2 + 3 =**

9. **2 + 4 =**

10. **3 + 4 =**

11. **4 + 4 =**

12. **7 + 2 =**

13. **4 + 5 =**

14. **1 + 4 =**

PRACTICE YOUR SUBTRACTION!

1. 4 -2 =

2. 9 - 2 =

3. 5 - 3 =

4. 10 - 5 =

5. 5 - 2 =

6. 3 - 1 =

7. 7 - 3 =

8. 8 - 3 =

9. 6 - 3 =

10. 6 - 2 =

11. 10 - 4 =

12. 7 - 5 =

13. 8 - 4 =

14. 8 - 2 =

ADVENTURES IN GEOMETRY

Trace the dotted line to divide these shapes into 2 equal parts. Then color one half (½) of the shape.

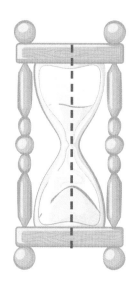

Trace the dotted line to divide these shapes into 4 equal parts. Then color in one quarter (¼) of each shape below.

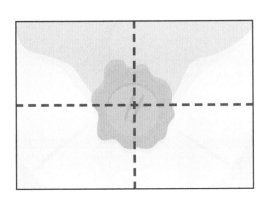

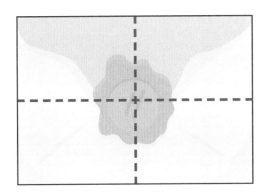

Color in one half of this magic chest:

Color in one quarter of this magic chest:

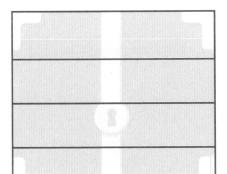

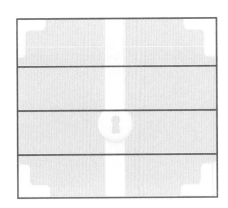

½

¼

WORD PROBLEMS

Read the problem carefully. Add or subtract to get the answer.

Example:

Ron learns 4 spells. He learns 2 new spells the next day and 3 more the next day. How many spells does he know in all?

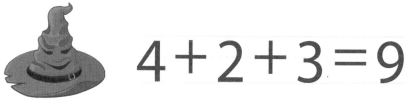

$$4+2+3=9$$

Answer: 9

1. Hufflepuff house gets 3 new students, Ravenclaw gets 5 new students, and Slytherin gets 2 new students. How many new students are there in all?

Answer:

2. Ollivanders has 16 wands to choose from. Hermione buys 2, Ron buys 2, and Harry buys 1. How many wands are left at the shop?

/ / / / / / / / / / / / / / / / /

Answer:

3. Hagrid finds 6 dragon eggs in the morning, 1 in the afternoon, and 0 at night. How many dragon eggs does he find in all?

Answer:

4. Harry starts the week with 20 broomsticks. Malfoy breaks 2 of them, Harry breaks 4 of them playing quidditch, and Ron trips over 2 more and breaks them. How many broomsticks does Harry have left?

Answer:

5. There are 15 spells in a spell book. 5 of them are advanced spells. 5 spells are intermediate spells. The rest are beginner spells. How many beginner spells are there?

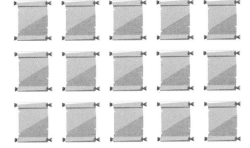

Answer:

6. There are 12 cats living at Hogwarts. Hermione takes her cat, Crookshanks, home. Filch's cat runs away. How many cats are left?

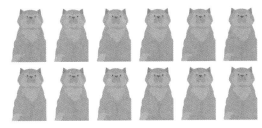

Answer:

HIPPOGRIFF'S GUIDE TO PLACE VALUE

Use the number on each hippogriff to fill in the place value chart.

Example:

Hundreds	Tens	Ones
2	5	6

1.

Hundreds	Tens	Ones

2.

Hundreds	Tens	Ones

3.

Hundreds	Tens	Ones

4.

Hundreds	Tens	Ones

5.

Hundreds	Tens	Ones

6.

Hundreds	Tens	Ones

HIGH COUNT CHALLENGE

Help the express train get to Hogwarts in time for wizard school to begin. Count from 110 to 125 to get it there.

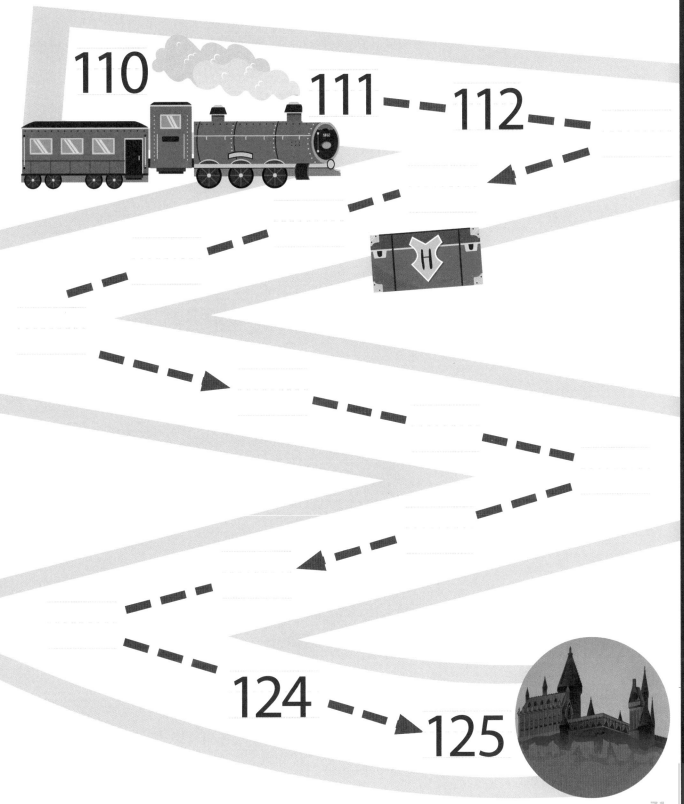

110 111 112

124 125

ODDS AND EVENS

Catch the flying keys by circling the ones with even numbers. You're one step closer to finding the Philosopher's Stone!

COUNTING MONEY

Harry needs a school uniform for his first year at Hogwarts. Count the money and help him get ready for wizard school!

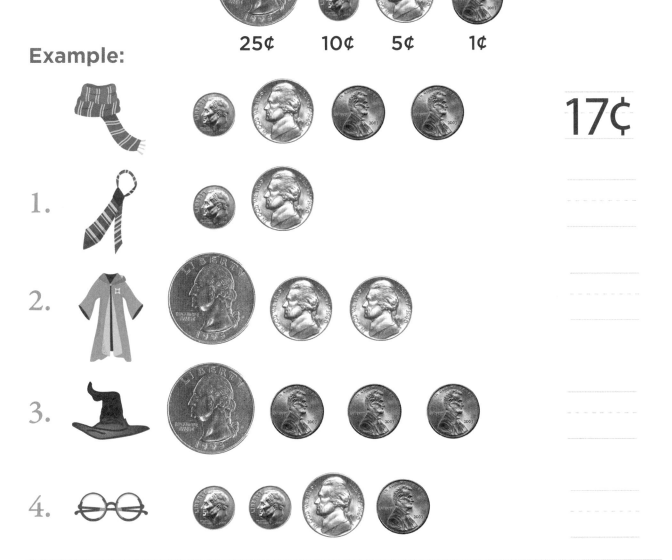

25¢ 10¢ 5¢ 1¢

Example:

17¢

1.

2.

3.

4.

WIZARD CHALLENGE: *Try this advanced problem!*

How much money does Harry need to buy all 5 of the items listed above? Add them up to find out!

Answer:

COUNT THE SHAPES

These gems spilled out of the House Point Hourglasses.
Count how many of each shape below.

1. Blue (Ravenclaw): ....

2. Red (Gryffindor): ....

3. Yellow (Hufflepuff): ....

4. Green (Slytherin): ....

WIZARD CHALLENGE: *Try this advanced problem!*
Which colored shapes above are octagons?

Answer:

Draw a wizard's castle below. Use as many shapes as you can. Add fun details and color!

CAULDRON ADDITION

Add the ones and then the tens to get the answer.

1.
$$\begin{array}{r} 40 \\ +25 \\ \hline \end{array}$$

2.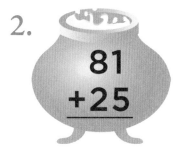
$$\begin{array}{r} 81 \\ +25 \\ \hline \end{array}$$

3.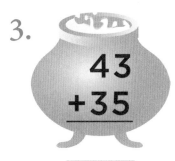
$$\begin{array}{r} 43 \\ +35 \\ \hline \end{array}$$

4.
$$\begin{array}{r} 22 \\ +64 \\ \hline \end{array}$$

5.
$$\begin{array}{r} 72 \\ +15 \\ \hline \end{array}$$

6.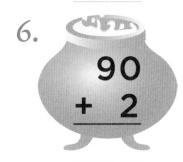
$$\begin{array}{r} 90 \\ +2 \\ \hline \end{array}$$

7.
$$\begin{array}{r} 83 \\ +11 \\ \hline \end{array}$$

8.
$$\begin{array}{r} 45 \\ +32 \\ \hline \end{array}$$

9.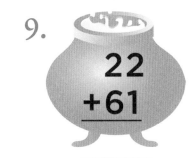
$$\begin{array}{r} 22 \\ +61 \\ \hline \end{array}$$

10.
$$\begin{array}{r} 16 \\ +73 \\ \hline \end{array}$$

11.
$$\begin{array}{r} 22 \\ +12 \\ \hline \end{array}$$

12.
$$\begin{array}{r} 51 \\ +54 \\ \hline \end{array}$$

MYSTERY MESSAGE

Subtract the ones, then the tens.
Use the letters to fill in the blanks
below and answer Ron's riddle.

45	89	93	27	52
− 32	− 45	− 32	− 12	− 11

F   Y   H   G   U

94	48	74	68	86
− 23	− 37	− 32	− 42	− 33

N   T   R   O   D

Q: How do you get into Gryffindor House?

Copy the letters from the answers above to find out!

                                           E

11 61 42 26 41 15 61   11 61

                         I   −

15 42 44 13 13   71

                !

53 26 26 42

BEAST BATTLE SHOWDOWN

Who would win in a battle? Compare the number of times each magical beast has struck the other using a greater than or less than symbol.

> Means Greater Than   < Means Less Than

Example: 385   <   392

1.   856   826

2.   445   454

3.   523   527

4.   672   607

5.   908   998

Who had the most wins? Circle the winner.

Hippogriff (Left Column)   **Basilisk (Right Column)**

SKIP COUNT CHALLENGE

Count by 3s to help the wizard chase away the dementor.

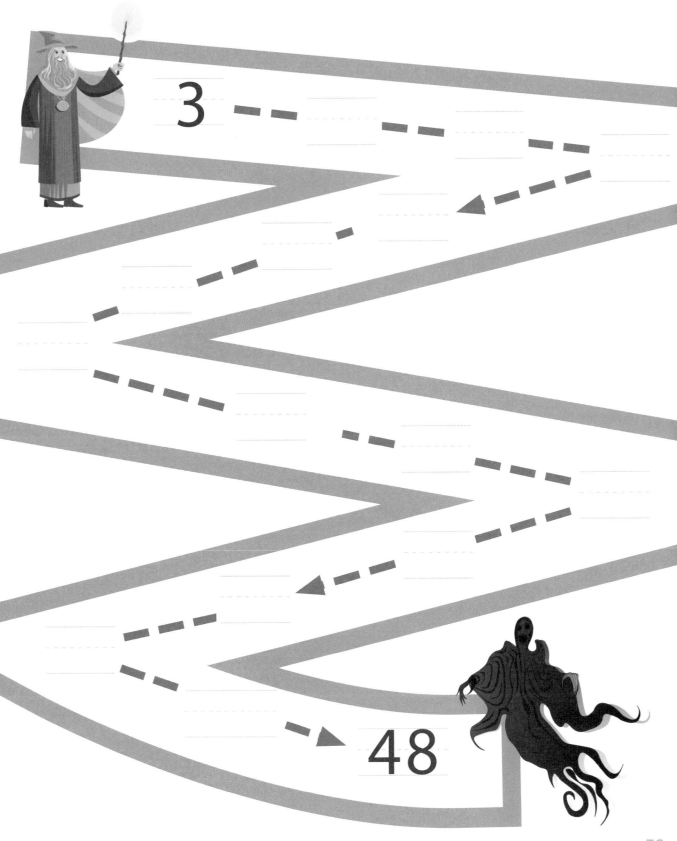

3

48

TELLING TIME

Look at the clocks below and write the time in the space provided:

Example:

Answer: **3:45**

1.

Answer: _____

2.

Answer: _____

3.

Answer: _____

4.

Answer: _____

5.

Answer: _____

6.

Answer: _____

7.

Answer: _____

8.

Answer: _____

9.

Answer: _____

10.

Answer: _____

11.

Answer: _____

12.

Answer: _____

13.

Answer: _____

ODDS AND EVENS

Today, you're the seeker, just like Harry! Circle all the golden snitches with odd numbers in order to catch them and win the quidditch game.

QUADRILATERAL CLASS

A wizard cast a spell on the quadrilaterals below and made them disappear. Outline their edges to make them reappear again!

Quadrilaterals are closed shapes with 4 sides. Squares and rectangles are two kinds of quadrilaterals.

MONSTER BOOK
MYSTERY NUMBER

There is a number hidden behind each Book of Monsters. Subtract or count on to figure out the mystery number!

Example: 15
+
_____
19

= **4**

1. 22
+
_____
29

=

2. 33
+
_____
53

=

3. 17
+
_____
25

=

4. 78
+
_____
82

=

5. 52
+
_____
64

=

6. 46
+
_____
56

=

7. 24
+
_____
30

=

8. 65
+
_____
70

=

MATH FACTS FOR MUGGLES

Solve the math equations below.

1. $6 + 3 =$

2. $4 + 3 =$

3. $1 + 8 =$

4. $3 + 5 =$

5. $3 + 2 =$

6. $6 + 4 =$

7. $10 - 3 =$

8. $10 - 7 =$

9. $7 - 4 =$

10. $6 - 1 =$

11. $9 - 4 =$

12. $6 - 3 =$

13. $10 - 2 =$

14. $3 + 3 =$

THE NIFFLER'S GUIDE TO PLACE VALUE

Identify the number that belongs in the place value chart and write it there.

Example:

Tens
8

1.

Hundreds

2.

Ones

3.

Hundreds

4.

Tens

5.

Ones

6.

Hundreds

SKIP COUNT CHALLENGE

Help Hagrid's baby dragon find its way back home. Count by 4s until you reach the dragon's mother.

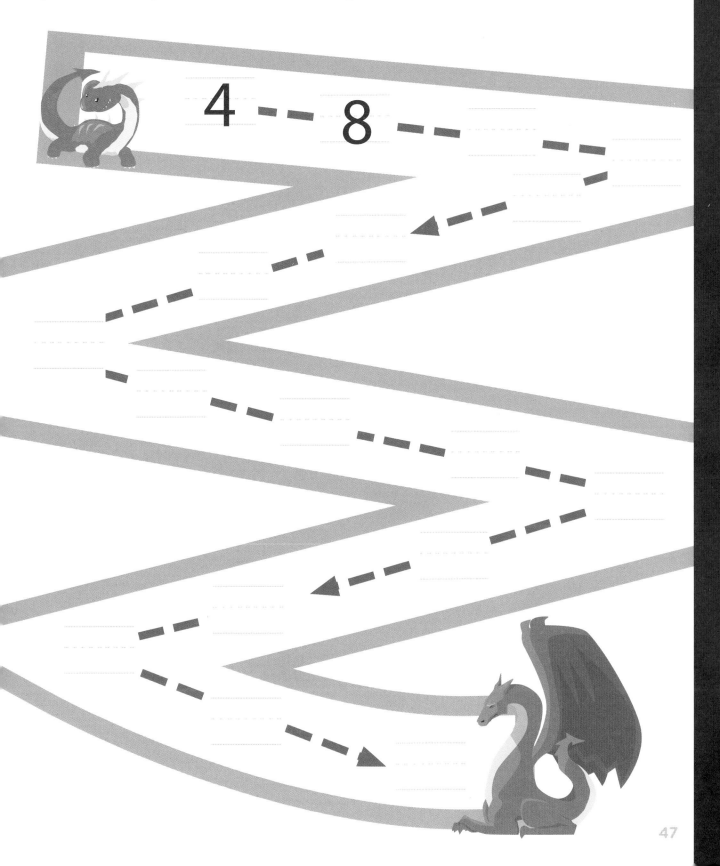

TALENT TALLY

Use the table to compare the number of charms and spells that each student knows.

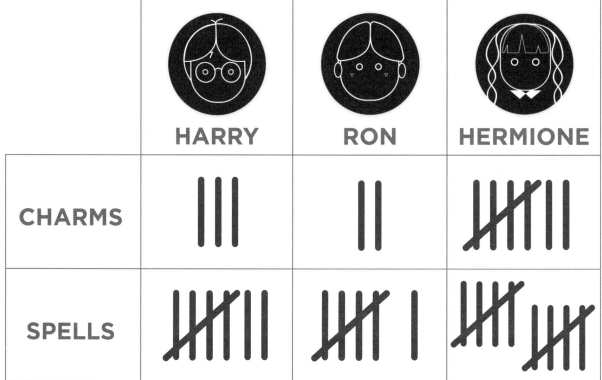

	HARRY	RON	HERMIONE
CHARMS	|||	||	ⅢⅠⅠ
SPELLS	||||	|||||	

1. How many charms does Hermione know?

2. Who knows more spells, Ron or Harry?

3. How many charms and spells does Hermione know in all?

4. How many more charms does Hermione know than Ron?

MAGICAL ITEM TALLY

Use the table to compare the magical items that Harry and Hermione own.

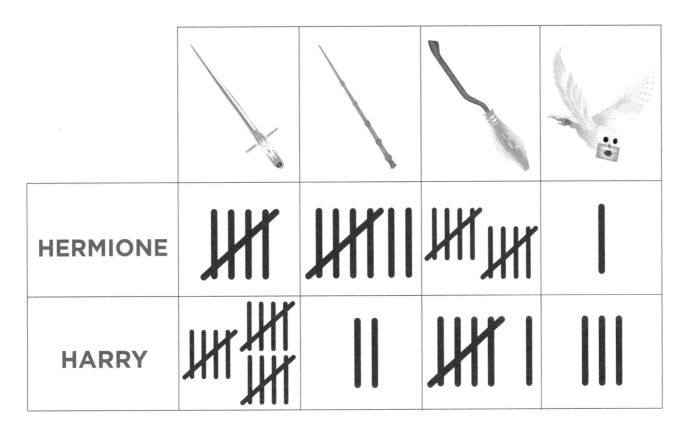

HERMIONE	卌 || 卌卌 ||	卌 卌		
HARRY	卌 卌 卌	||	卌		|||

1. How many wands does Hermione own?

2. Harry and Hermione both have lots of broomsticks. How many **more** broomsticks does Hermione have?

3. Harry and Hermione both have swords. How many **more** swords does Harry have?

4. Who has the most messenger owls?

MATH FACTS FOR MUGGLES

Solve the math facts equations below.

PRACTICE YOUR ADDITION!

1. 3 + 3 =

2. 5 + 4 =

3. 9 + 1 =

4. 6 + 2 =

5. 4 + 2 =

6. 2 + 3 =

7. 5 + 5 =

8. 3 + 3 =

9. 2 + 7 =

10. 1 + 5 =

11. 4 + 4 =

12. 10 + 0 =

13. 1 + 1 =

14. 2 + 5 =

PRACTICE YOUR SUBTRACTION!

1. 7 - 3 =

2. 5 - 4 =

3. 9 - 1 =

4. 6 - 2 =

5. 4 - 2 =

6. 8 - 3 =

7. 5 - 5 =

8. 3 - 1 =

9. 10 - 7 =

10. 5 - 2 =

11. 9 - 4 =

12. 10 - 0 =

13. 8 - 6 =

14. 7 - 5 =

WORD PROBLEMS

Write a number sentence to help you solve these word problems.

Example: Harry sees 15 flying keys. He catches 6 in one hand and 3 in the other. How many keys are left?

15 - 6 - 3 = 6

Answer: **6 keys**

1. Ron has four classes a day for three days. How many classes does he have in all?

Answer:

2. In one day, Harry is chased by 3 dementors, 4 trolls, and 1 snake. How many creatures are chasing him?

Answer:

3. Ginny has 6 Nimbus 2000 broomsticks. Harry gives her 1 Firebolt broomstick. She gets 2 more from her family. How many broomsticks does Ginny have in all?

Answer:

4. Harry faces Voldemort once when he is a baby. He faces him 3 more times as a young child. Harry faces him 1 last time as a teenager. How many times does Harry face Voldemort?

Answer:

5. Dumbledore eats 4 of Harry's flavor beans. The next day he eats 2 more. That night, Harry offers him his last flavor bean. How many of Harry's flavor beans does Dumbledore eat?

Answer:

HARRY'S GUIDE TO PLACE VALUE

Match the number on Harry's uniform to the place value descriptions on the right.

Example:

342 → Tens: **4**

1.

651 → Ones

2.

742 → Tens

3.

329 → Ones

4.

810 → Hundreds

5.

563 → Tens

6.

239 → Hundreds

SKIP COUNT CHALLENGE

Count by 100s to help the owl deliver an important message.

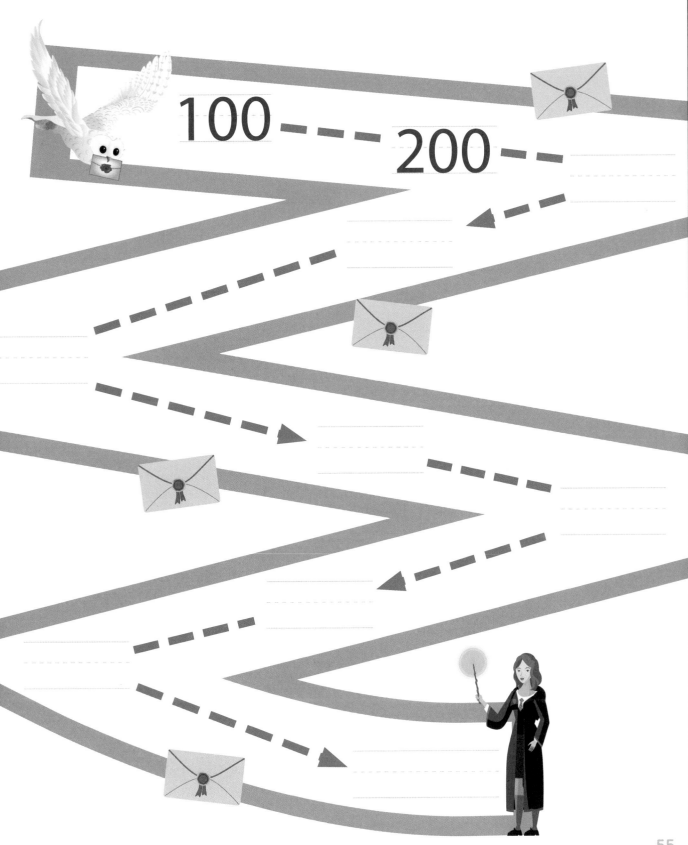

100

200

TELLING TIME

Look at the clocks below and write the time in the space provided:

Example:

Answer: **4:15**

1.

Answer: _____

2.

Answer: _____

3.

Answer: _____

4.

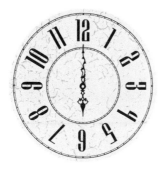

Answer: _____

5.

Answer: _____

COUNTING MONEY

How much money is hidden in each treasure chest? Add up the coins to find out.

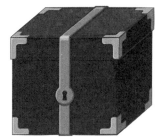

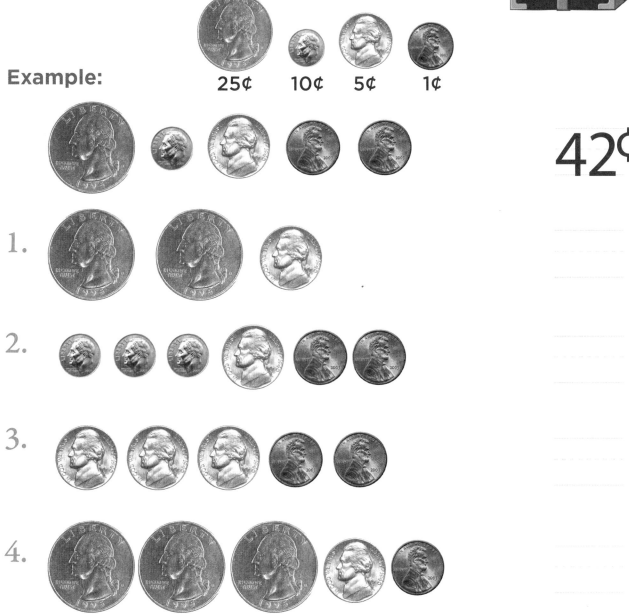

Example:

25¢   10¢   5¢   1¢

42¢

1.

2.

3.

4.

===

WIZARD CHALLENGE: *Try this advanced problem!*

Hermione goes to the Magical Menagerie with 6 coins in her pocket that add up to 30¢. There is only 1 kind of coin in her pocket. What coin is it?

WIZARD SCHOOL OF GEOMETRY

This magical scroll is divided into 4 equal parts called fourths. Color the magical scroll below according to the description.

1. Color: One Fourth

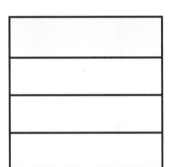

¹⁄₄

2. Color: Three Fourths

³⁄₄

3. Color: Two Fourths

²⁄₄

4. Color: Four Fourths

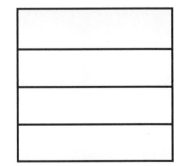

⁴⁄₄

In order to enter the secret chamber, you must match the image of castle stones at left to the correct fraction on the right.

Example:

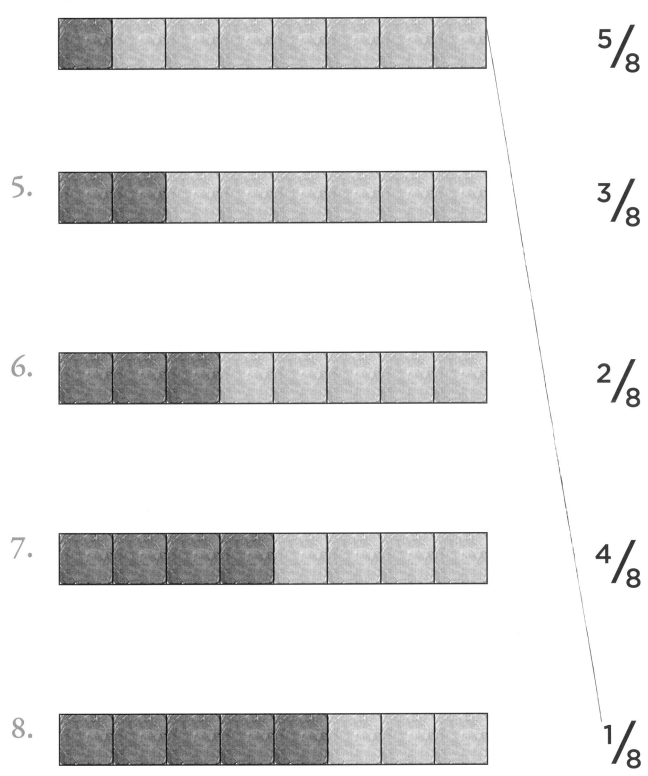

5.

6.

7.

8.

5/8

3/8

2/8

4/8

1/8

ANSWER KEY

Page 4: Addition By Grouping
1. 16
2. 32
3. 21
4. 15

Page 5: Mystery Message
3	6
11	15
2	7
13	14
	10

A: Because they are
DOUBLE CROSSERS

Page 6: Harry's Guide to Place Value
1. 4 tens 2 ones
2. 3 tens 5 ones
3. 3 tens 7 one
4. 1 ten 8 ones
5. 4 tens 4 ones
6. 2 tens 9 ones

Page 7: Skip Count Challenge
2, 4, 6, 8, 10, 12, 14 ,16, 18, 20, 22, 24, 26, 28

Page 8: Telling Time
1. 8:30
2. 10:15
3. 5:30
4. 1:00
5. 7:30

Page 9: Counting Money
1. 18¢
2. 26¢
3. 80¢
4. 22¢
5. 35¢
6. 54¢

Wizard Challenge: 9 nickels

Page 10-11: Adventures in Geometry
Note: Answers may vary.

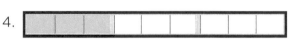

3. 9

Wizard Challenge:

A. $\frac{1}{2}$

Page 12-13: Word Problems
1. 4 friends
2. 2 mandrakes
3. 4 spell books
4. 9 pairs
5. 8 letters
6. 5 dragons
7. 5 more cauldrons

Page 14: Wizard's Guide to Place Value

1.
Tens	Ones
1	8

2.
Tens	Ones
2	5

3.
Tens	Ones
2	7

4.
Tens	Ones
1	3

5.
Tens	Ones
3	9

6.
Tens	Ones
2	3

Page 15: Skip Count Challenge
5, 10, 15, 20, 25, 30, 35, 40, 45, 50, 55, 60, 65

Page 16: Time for Magic
1. G   2. F   3. C
4. A   5. B   6. D

Page 17: Telling Time

1.
4:30

2.
2:00

3.
7:30

4.
10:15

5.
5:30

Page 18: Learning About Shapes

1. C
2. A
3. D
4. B

Page 19: Find the Shapes

5. Circle, Triangle (C, T)
6. Rectangle (R)
7. Rectangle, Circle, Triangle (R, C, T)
Wizard Challenge: *Answers may vary.*

Page 20: Addition by Grouping

1. 32
2. 26
3. 28

Page 21: Mystery Message

19
3
14
17
13
15
11
8
7
A: HE HAD NO BODY TO GO WITH

Page 22: The Triwizard Cup Challenge

1. E   2. B   3. A   4. C

Page 23: Skip Count Challenge

10, 20, 30, 40, 50, 60, 70, 80, 90, 100, 110, 120, 130, 140

Page 24-25: Math Facts for Muggles

Page 24		Page 25	
1.	10	1.	2
2.	7	2.	7
3.	8	3.	2
4.	8	4.	5
5.	10	5.	3
6.	9	6.	2
7.	10	7.	4
8.	5	8.	5
9.	6	9.	3
10.	7	10.	4
11.	8	11.	6
12.	9	12.	2
13.	9	13.	4
14.	5	14.	6

Page 26-27: Adventures in Geometry

Note: Answers may vary.

½   ¼

Page 28-29: Word Problems

1. 10 new students
2. 11 wands
3. 7 dragon eggs
4. 12 broomsticks
5. 5 beginner spells
6. 10 cats

Page 30: Hippogriff's Guide to Place Value

1. Hundreds: 3 Tens: 6 Ones: 0
2. Hundreds: 4 Tens: 9 Ones: 2
3. Hundreds: 5 Tens: 8 Ones: 4
4. Hundreds: 3 Tens: 4 Ones: 2
5. Hundreds: 8 Tens: 5 Ones: 6
6. Hundreds: 6 Tens: 5 Ones: 3

Page 31: High Count Challenge

110, 111, 112, 113, 114, 115, 116, 117, 118, 119, 120, 121, 122, 123, 124, 125.

Page 32: Odds and Evens

Page 33: Counting Money

1. 15¢
2. 35¢
3. 28¢
4. 26¢

Wizard Challenge: $1.21

Page 34: Count the Shapes

1. 6
2. 7
3. 7
4. 5

Wizard Challenge: The green and blue shapes are octagons.

Page 35: Count the Shapes (continued)

Answers may vary.

Page 36: Cauldron Addition

1. 65
2. 106
3. 78
4. 86
5. 87
6. 92
7. 94
8. 77
9. 83
10. 89
11. 34
12. 105

Page 37: Mystery Message

13, 44, 61, 15, 41, 71, 11, 42, 26, 53

A: THROUGH THE GRYFFIN-DOOR!

Page 38: Beast Battle Showdown

1. >
2. <
3. <
4. >
5. <

The basilisk is the winner.

Page 39: Skip Count Challenge

3, 6, 9, 12, 15, 18, 21, 24, 27, 30, 33, 36, 39, 42, 45, 48

Page 40-41: Telling Time

1. 4:15
2. 6:10
3. 8:25
4. 3:50
5. 1:55
6. 12:40
7. 9:05
8. 6:45
9. 2:35
10. 1:10
11. 10:25
12. 5:55
13. 6:40

Page 42: Odds and Evens

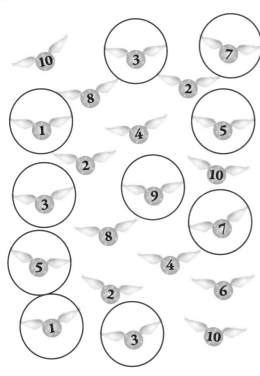

Page 43: Quadrilateral Class

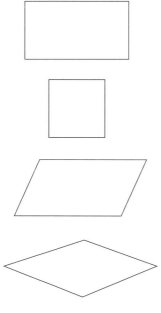

Page 44: Monster Book Mystery Number

1. 7
2. 20
3. 8
4. 4
5. 12
6. 10
7. 6
8. 5

Page 45: Math Facts for Muggles

1. 9
2. 7
3. 9
4. 8
5. 5
6. 10
7. 7
8. 3
9. 3
10. 5
11. 5
12. 3
13. 8
14. 6

Page 46: The Niffler's Guide to Place Value

1. 6
2. 3
3. 8
4. 3
5. 2
6. 1

Page 47: Skip Count Challenge

4, 8, 12, 16, 20, 24, 28, 32, 36, 40, 44, 48, 52, 56, 60, 64

Page 48: Talent Tally

1. Hermione knows 7 charms.
2. Harry knows more spells than Ron.
3. Hermione knows 17 charms and spells.
4. Hermione knows 5 more charms than Ron.

Page 49: Magical Item Tally
1. Hermione owns 7 wands.
2. Hermione owns 4 more broomsticks.
3. Harry has 10 more swords.
4. Harry has the most messenger owls.

Page 50-51: Math Facts for Muggles

Page 50	Page 51
1. 6	1. 4
2. 9	2. 1
3. 10	3. 8
4. 8	4. 4
5. 6	5. 2
6. 5	6. 5
7. 10	7. 0
8. 6	8. 2
9. 9	9. 3
10. 6	10. 3
11. 8	11. 5
12. 10	12. 10
13. 2	13. 2
14. 7	14. 2

Page 52-53: Word Problems
1. 4+4+4= 12 classes
2. 3+4+1= 8 creatures
3. 6+1+2= 9 broomsticks
4. 1+3+1= 5 times
5. 4+2+1= 7 flavor beans

Page 54: Harry's Guide to Place Value
1. 1
2. 4
3. 9
4. 8
5. 6
6. 2

Page 55: Skip Count Challenge
100, 200, 300, 400, 500, 600, 700, 800, 900, 1,000

Page 56: Telling Time
1. 2:25   2. 7:50
3. 6:05   4. 6:00
5. 1:15

Page 57: Counting Money
1. 55¢
2. 37¢
3. 17¢
4. 81¢
Wizard Challenge: Nickel

Page 58: Wizard School of Geometry
Note: Answers may vary.

Page 59: Wizard School of Geometry (continued)

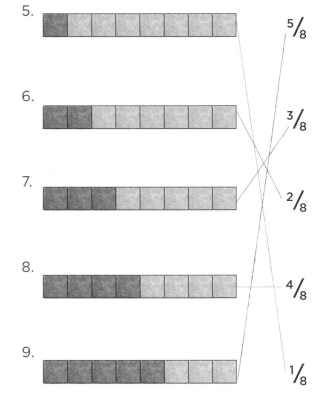